# Life After Abortion

## HEALING AND RESTORATION FOR WOMEN HURT BY ABORTION

## Ann Taylor

Publisher Ann Taylor

Copyright © 2016 by Ann Taylor

All Rights Reserved. No part of this publication may be reproduced, stored in a retrieval system, or transmitted in any form or by any means – electronic, mechanical, photocopy, recording, or any other – except for brief quotations in printed reviews, without the prior permission of the author.

Scriptures have been taken from the New King James Version. Copyright © 1982 by Thomas Nelson, Inc. Used by permission. All rights reserved.

* Some names and details, in the testimonies shared, have been changed to protect the identity of persons involved.

Life After Abortion/ Ann Taylor. —1st edition
ISBN 978-0-9953779-0-5

# Contents

In The Beginning ............................................................. 11
Australia Here We Come ................................................. 13
The Surprise .................................................................... 17
Supernatural Intervention ................................................. 19
God's Grace in a Time of Loss ......................................... 23
The Nightmares ............................................................... 27
The Survivors .................................................................. 31
Redemptive Healing ........................................................ 43
The Light at the End of the Tunnel ................................... 57
A Word to Christian Women ............................................ 67

## Dedication

I dedicate this book to Jason, the son I lost

To Mikaela, the daughter I almost lost

And to all the brave women who have told their story

# ACKNOWLEDGEMENTS

My grateful thanks and appreciation goes to my dear friend Karen Skinner, without whose help, encouragement, love and support, I would not even have begun this project. She has freely given her valuable time, advice and technical expertise, in an effort to help me get this book into the hands of those who need it. Thank you Karen.

My love and admiration and heartfelt thanks goes to each and every one of the women who shared their hearts and stories with me. They trusted me to write their stories that others may read them and find healing. Thank you ladies.

My grateful appreciation goes to Julie Harriman for her expert eye, patience and ability to correct all my grammatical errors. You have done a wonderful job Julie. Thank you.

Many thanks to Doug Skinner for his wonderful photographic ability. Doug is responsible for my front cover and picture of me. Thank you Doug.

Much love and thanks to my husband Bob, who had so often to endure being my sounding board. Thank You my darling.

My greatest appreciation and thankfulness goes to my wonderful Lord Jesus who not only inspired me to write this book, but gave me the ability to do it. Rom 8:28 says, "All things work together for good for those that love God, those whom He has called according to His purposes".

Only God can take all the mess-ups in our lives and use them for His glorious purposes.

We give Him our ashes and He gives us His beauty.

Thank you my Lord.

## Endorsements

An inspiring story as can only be told by one who has walked that journey. As you read this book, you will be moved and impacted as you witness God's ability to bring forth beauty out of ashes. A story of hope, faith and love, where God turns it all around.

## Ps Jimmy Njino, Senior Pastor, Victory Life Toowoomba

When I first read this book, I was tremendously amazed by Ann's personal story. 'Life After Abortion' is filled with true, untainted stories from women who had been through such events. It shares the secrets of pressing past previous guilt, and pressing forward in Christ Jesus. This book is a must read for all. It will give you a new perspective as to the gift of life.

## Ruth Chai-Njino

It is a delight to see lives transformed by the love of God, even after a traumatic event like abortion. Thankfully, it is possible to move on and no longer be crippled by the past. In her book, 'Life After Abortion', Ann compassionately encourages the reader to choose the path of life and indicates the way to experience freedom from their past. Ann clearly shows an understanding from her own personal journey as she deals with both perspectives of abortion – the mother and the unborn child. This is a must read for any woman who has experienced abortion or even considering it!

## David & Julie Harriman, Prayer Counsellors, Victory Life Toowoomba

Ann has put into words the quiet desperation of pregnant women, either being coerced to abort their babies or feeling a hopelessness that abortion is the 'only' answer, leaving mothers baby-less and lost. Her book, though, is uplifting. Ann draws post-abortive mothers' hearts from this pit of sadness and despair, to know that there is a loving God just waiting to forgive and heal them - no-one is beyond redemption. We know this book will help women find the path to healing and wholeness once again.

## Teresa Martin, State President, Cherish Life Queensland

You will be encouraged as you step inside the pages of this book and as you hear the testimony of a woman who found hope and purpose in the midst of a world where she thought aborting her unborn child was the only answer. She went from a place of absolute hope deferred where her life was sick, to a place where desire and the will to keep living sprang up as a tree of life within her. As you read this small but powerful book, dare to believe that you also will begin to see light penetrate into every dark place, and bring hope into the midst of your world.

## Ps Chris McDonald, Associate Pastor, Victory Life Toowoomba

The topic of abortion is a paradoxical inconvenient truth in today's society. Few are the voices that dare to give true evidential facts of the detrimental effects this choice represents to many who take the termination option.

Ann Taylor is one of those few voices who willingly, through her own experience, dares to express and bring to the forefront the psychological, emotional, multigenerational repercussions of terminations, as well as effects of failed termination attempts.

Furthermore, through the stories featured in Ann's book, a virtually untouched microcosm of thousands upon thousands of women's disconnect with the real source of their demise, is bravely exposed.

There could not be a better time to commence to engage in a true veridic discourse of the unrecognized grief and mental distress a termination causes in many women. Women need to know that grief is grief regardless of circumstances around the activating event.

Moreover, women and men who have been participants in terminations need to know, and have planted in their hearts, that there is a redeemer who makes all things new. As willing and able as He was to forgive the adulterous, the thief and the murderer over two thousand years ago, He is just as willing today to do it again; that includes post-abortive women and men.

He is waiting with open arms and willing to carry and take away the suffering in their souls.

Jesus is His name!

**Luz Miranda, Counsellor – Priceless Life. B. Soc. Sci. Counselling**

## Introduction

Does our beginning in life determine our end? Certainly our beginnings greatly affect many aspects of our life, but our fate is not sealed by where we started. Rather, it's the choices we make that will determine where we finish.

Life is full of choices. We make them every day. Some good, some not so good and some so bad that they fill us with regret.

Marrying my first husband was my number one major regret at that time. The old saying, 'jumping out of the frypan and into the fire', fitted my situation perfectly.

I was born and raised in Coventry, England in a somewhat strange household. By strange I mean, we lived with my grandmother, the matriarch of the family, along with mum's three elder unmarried brothers and her divorced sister with her young son. Each one rather eccentric in their own way, all neatly compacted into a small two-bedroom house with an attic.

Mum was deemed the black sheep of the family. She had had a baby out of wedlock which was considered a shameful thing in those days. As a child, I felt the animosity against her from the rest of the family. I was too young to understand, but somehow I always felt her shame, like it belonged to me too. We seemed to be inferior to everyone else.

We were assigned the 'attic' which was the cause of my many nightmares for years to come. I was eight when we finally moved from that house after two of the brothers and the sister married. There still weren't enough bedrooms or even beds in the new house for me to have one of my own. Consequently, I shared a bed with my mum till I was seventeen before running away, escaping as I thought.

In spite of any lack that I may have had, I knew that my family really loved me and did all they could to care for me. Problem was, in my naivety, I felt they over protected me to the point of suffocation.

I had met Michael a year or so before, but with all the restrictions that were put upon me, mainly by my grandmother and uncle, we'd only had stolen time together. But I was in love, or so I thought, with this worldly, adventurous seaman. I was eighteen when we married, with my head full of dreams of a bright and beautiful future. But, it wasn't very long before the dreams seemed more like nightmares and suddenly, that 'fire' made the 'frypan' look pretty good. Oh, how I longed to turn back the clock – but too late, too late.

The choices we make! Some good, some not so good and some we live to regret.

This book is about those choices.

Without a doubt, the best choice I ever made was to make Jesus the Lord and Savior of my life. Since that time, He has brought Peace that passes understanding into the storms of my life. He has shone His brilliant light into my darkness and dispersed it. I have found healing in Him from things I never thought would be, or even could be, healed. He has turned around the devastating results of some of those bad choices that I have made in my life, and somehow has managed to miraculously bring good out of them.

He longs to do the same for you.

CHAPTER 1

# In The Beginning

If only I knew then what I know now. I wonder how many of us have pondered that thought. But then, if I had known, and not lived through the circumstances of that time, I would not have a story to tell. The purpose in my story is that others may know now what I did not know then, and that their story would have a happy ending.

Over the years, whenever I've shared events from my past, people have often commented, "You should write a book." Well here I am at last, perhaps the first of many books. This story is about one small but important portion of my past. To bring proper clarity to that portion, I need to include certain aspects of my life leading up to that time.

I was eighteen when I married Michael, my first husband. I was young, naive, and very foolish. Michael was a seaman, which seemed so romantic at the time, listening to tales of his exploits and the countries he'd visited. But, reality set in not long after we got married. I discovered, with much pain and great anguish, that Michael was an alcoholic, a gambler, an unfaithful womanizer and, an abuser to boot.

I felt trapped. Escape was out of the question. I came from a family whose philosophies were, 'you've made your bed, now lie in it', and, 'that marriage was for life, no matter what'. I could hardly turn to them, especially since I wanted them to be proud of me. I never seemed to quite measure up. I suffered greatly from rejection which drove me to relentlessly seek the approval of man.

I became pregnant four months after we married and rather than being the joy it should have been, it just seemed to further tighten the trap.

As time went on, Michael grew more and more controlling, manipulative and possessive. I felt as though he lived my life as well as his. I had no identity of my own left. Who was I? I didn't seem to know anymore.

CHAPTER 2

# Australia Here We Come

Eight years went by. We now had three children, two girls and a boy.

Those years were filled with so much pain and torment. I felt that the only good thing about that time was my children.

Our lives reached a crisis point in 1973. Michael had re-mortgaged the house several times to accommodate his gambling habit. We could no longer afford the repayments, so our only option was to sell. We owed so much to the bank that they would get most of the profit from the sale, so buying again would be impossible.

What would we do? Where would we live? Those were some of the anxious questions plaguing my mind. The answer came in a series of inspirations and ideas.

One day whilst washing up, gazing aimlessly out of the kitchen window, worrying about the lack of prospects before us, I heard a voice clearly say, "Go to Australia". It made me jump it seemed to be so loud and clear.

I did not dare think, at that time, that it could possibly be God speaking to me. I mean, who was I that God would speak to me? These days I know only too well that God does speak to us. Not always as loudly and clearly as He spoke to me that day, but He does speak to us in various ways because He loves us and we are important to Him; He's interested in all of our circumstances. He longs for us to give Him access into our lives so He can make a difference.

Australia had been the country that Michael had visited many times when he was in the Merchant Navy. He had told me so much about this beautiful country that he'd grown to love, that I had developed a deep desire to see it for myself. Australia held a special place in my heart. Years before (I was sixteen at the time) Michael and I had planned to elope. He was going to join a ship going to Australia and I was going to stow away in his cabin till we arrived there, then we would 'jump ship' as the term went. People actually used to do that and perhaps still do.

It may only have been a childish dream at the time.

Or maybe, it was a sense of destiny.

Mysteriously, at the same time that I heard that voice telling me to "Go to Australia", ads appeared in local newspapers, calling for people to immigrate to Australia.

One of the jobs they were advertising was for foundry workers for BHP. This was so providential because Michael had actually worked in a foundry before and so had the required experience.

We attended an introduction night at Town Hall where we watched a film about Australia. That film fostered an even deeper affection in me for a country I'd only ever seen in my mind's eye before.

We set the ball rolling by sending in our application. Within a couple of weeks, we had an interview in Birmingham. They were very encouraging, but said the processing would take several months. This suited us fine since we still hadn't sold the house.

We were so excited that it seemed to put a new lease of life into our marriage. It was to be a new start for us and Michael promised that things would be different.

He had everything worked out. We would both get jobs when we got to Australia and we would save hard and buy a house. Everything was going to be so wonderful.

CHAPTER 3

# The Surprise

A couple of weeks later, a surprise discovery seemed to put a spanner in the works. I realized I was pregnant.

When I related the news to Michael, his response was so 'disproportionate'. He was so angry; you'd have thought I managed to get pregnant all by myself. He raved on and on about how this would spoil all the plans we'd made, and we could not allow that to happen. His next statement jolted me. He told me he wanted me to have an abortion!

I knew nothing about abortion, except it was the way to become 'un-pregnant'. But the more I questioned it, the more insistent he became.

Michael used his usual manipulative methods to convince me it was no big deal; it would be for the best. He suggested I talk to his mother about it, since he knew that she had had an abortion. I went to talk with his mother and she informed me that she had had more than one abortion and there was nothing to it. It wasn't a baby yet anyway, only a mass of cells, tissue and blood vessels.

I was ready to believe all of this, not knowing anything different. Above all, I wanted to please Michael. I didn't want to lose what I thought we'd found.

A few days later, I went to see the doctor that I'd been referred to. He asked me a few simple questions, which were designed to determine the state of my sanity. Satisfied that I was of sound mind, he agreed to organize the abortion. In less than a week, I received a letter in the mail telling me to present myself at the hospital in two weeks' time, which would make me almost three months pregnant.

I was amazed at how easy it was.


Not once did the doctor offer any explanation about the procedure or give me any insight as to what would happen.

But the truth was, I didn't ask! So convinced was I that this was 'no big deal'.

CHAPTER 4

# Supernatural Intervention

I busied myself that morning, getting together the things the letter had said for me to take with me to the hospital. It was the day before I was due to go in. Apparently, I would be in and out on the same day. Pregnant when I went in, and not pregnant when I came out.

Had I really stopped to ponder that thought? I really don't remember what I was thinking about that day. Likely, there were a mixture of thoughts going on in my head, like the weight of the debt hanging over us, the excitement of going to Australia and the promised new start, trying to sell the house and the timing of everything falling into place.

One underlying thought that was always on my mind, and that was how to please an unpleasable husband.

I never gave up trying, and what I was about to do the next day was another attempt.

That evening Michael left on his usual trip to the local pub.

Though I've strained trying to remember the details of that night, the memory remains hazy and illusive, as though just out of my reach somehow. The only thing I remember with certainty is that I became so ill and incapacitated that I couldn't get up out of the chair I was sitting in to let Michael in when he got home. He somehow broke in and found me 'seemingly hallucinating', repeating over and over again, "God doesn't want me to get rid of this baby".

But I wasn't hallucinating. I'd never been more certain of anything in my life before.

At the time, I didn't understand what had happened to me. I realize now that Almighty God had somehow touched me and divinely intervened.

Something had switched on, on the inside of me, like a light dispelling the darkness.

This was a baby inside of me, my baby, and I wanted this baby to live and be born.

Unfortunately, Michael was equally determined that I would go ahead with the planned abortion.

The next day though, because I was still so very ill, they cancelled the procedure, promising they would re-schedule as soon as possible.

I was four months pregnant when they made the next appointment. By this time, I'd truly fallen in love with this tiny being that was growing on the inside of me.

Michael was very determined that I would keep that appointment. Even though I had continually pleaded with him, he had ignored every plea with his own twisted form of logic.

He forced me to go to the hospital with him that morning, I got as far as getting undressed and getting into the bed. All the time, I couldn't stop the river of tears from rolling down my cheeks.

It was a small room with three other women in their beds, all with their eyes fixed on me. They were there, I presumed, for the very same purpose that I was.

Looking back on that day, I've realized that those women were in the same place that I had been before I'd had my supernatural encounter. This is the same for thousands and thousands of other women who were and are believing a lie they are ignorant to, or ignoring the facts.

I sat there in that hospital bed feeling absolute desperation, crying out from my heart to somehow be rescued from this situation.

Suddenly, without any warning, I watched as Michael's countenance dramatically changed; as though some sort of transformation had occurred on the inside of his brain. He turned to me and said, "Get up and get dressed, we're going home!" I couldn't believe my ears, but I hurriedly got out of that bed and threw on my clothes for fear he'd change his mind.

I knew it wasn't my tears that had moved him, as I'd cried bucket loads over the past month or more, whilst pleading with him.

No, this was another *divine* intervention.

From that moment on, abortion was never mentioned again.

I went on to have a beautiful little girl, whom we named Mikaela Ann.

She was born here in Australia two months after we arrived.

Is this the end of my story? Far from it!

There are ramifications that come with abortion and even attempted ones.

In my preparations for writing this book, I have done a great deal of research and have been blown away, time and again, as to how far reaching some of those consequences have been. Consequences not restricted to the mothers alone, but even to the siblings and many fathers of aborted babies.

My heart goes out to those mothers who have had abortions. I know that many of them would have been as deceived as I was into believing that the baby within them was nothing more than tissue and cells. I also believe every one of them suffer from a deep sense of loss, guilt, shame and grief. Many have turned to alcohol or drugs in an effort to dull the pain. Some have attempted suicide and some, perhaps, even succeeded.

It's a secret world that society knows nothing about, because its hidden behind a veil of shame and pain. They're the walking wounded that hide their pain for fear of being misunderstood and judged. God's heart aches for these women; He longs to heal their pain.

I have interviewed some of these precious women who have kindly shared their stories with me, some of which I will include.

My aim is to bring hope and peace to the ones who desperately need it, and to take the privilege of shining the light upon a pathway that will bring lasting peace and complete healing to those who wish to take it.

CHAPTER 5

# God's Grace in a Time of Loss

Mikaela was less than six months old when Jason, my son who was two, became really sick. We'd been in Australia seven months by now and he had been unwell most of that time. But then, so were all the other children in the Commonwealth Hostel where we were living. All the childhood diseases went around like wildfire there. Though Jason seemed to be getting worse rather than better, no one seemed to have any real answers as to why.

He was admitted to the local hospital who then sent us to Camperdown Children's Hospital in Sydney for more tests. The tests showed that Jason had a large brain tumor at the base of his skull. He had a build-up of fluid that was putting a lot of pressure on his brain and they had to do a small operation immediately to release the pressure.

They intended to let him recover for a couple of weeks before doing the main operation to remove the tumor, but during the night he hemorrhaged and they had to operate straight away.

We were staying at the Sydney hostel at the time and were woken up in the early hours of the morning and told to get to the hospital immediately. That was when the full impact of the seriousness of the situation hit me full force.

Up until that moment, I hadn't realized that there was any danger of losing him.

I had been so distracted with Michael's behavior, whilst trying to care for a sick child, a young baby and the girls. The realization hadn't registered till that moment.

Life had been bad enough in England, but at least there was family there. Not that I availed myself much of them, but just the comfort in knowing that they were there if I really needed them. Now here we were in a strange country with no one to turn to. Fear and panic rose up so much so I struggled to breathe, and my heart was pounding so hard it felt like it would explode from my chest.

Once again Michael and I were united by a common cause for a while; this time it was fear and heartache.

The operation took several hours and then, for almost two weeks, Jason lay unconscious and motionless on a hospital bed with various tubes and machines attached to him.

The hospital staff were very kind in getting the other children cared for so that we could spend every minute with Jason. It was the most traumatic two weeks of our lives. I was afraid to leave him, even to go to the bathroom, in the fear that he might die while I was away.

It all happened over the Easter holiday, which meant it took longer for them to get test results back.

One evening, Jason's breathing suddenly changed; it became loud and wheezy. There happened to be a lung specialist on the ward at that time attending to someone else, so the nurse called him to look at Jason. Next minute, there were several doctors around his bed and we were asked to wait outside. Half an hour later, the surgeon who had operated on Jason came and asked to speak with us and we were taken to a small room. He firstly told us that Jason had pneumonia, which was always a risk under the circumstances. He then explained that when they operated they had found that the tumor had infiltrated through his brain, and that consequently, they had only taken out what they were able to get at. They had only received the results from pathology that day to say that the tumor was malignant. His advice to us was to let him go quietly and quickly with the pneumonia. The alternative, even if they were able to cure the pneumonia, was that he would still die, sooner or later without ever regaining consciousness.

He left the decision in our hands, and made the choice sound ever so simple, but of course it was not.

Three agonizing days later Jason was dead.

If ever I thought I knew what pain was in the past, nothing could compare with what I was feeling now. No words are sufficient to describe the agony of loss. The suddenness of it adds to the confusion of emotions. To have and hold a child one minute, and the next, nothing but emptiness.

It was only with the passing of time, a long time, that I realized the 'grace' of God. At first though, there was a period of time when a lie tormented my mind. Did God take my son because I was going to abort my daughter?

Through the agony of that time, I came to know this wonderful God as my Lord and Savior, and I now know, without any doubt, that it is not in God's character to torment us or make us pay, as we are sometimes convinced to believe.

God is love, and every thought and action towards us is motivated by His love for us. In spite of the wrong things that we do, if we will only turn to Him, He longs to show us His grace and mercy.

It was His wonderful grace and mercy that He had extended towards me. There was less than a year between the planned abortion of Mikaela and the death of Jason.

I can only imagine the **magnification** of all the pain I was now suffering if I had lost Mikaela too. And except for the divine intervention of God, that would have been the case. Oh, the wonderful grace of God! As it was, thanks to Him, I had Mikaela to cuddle and hold, as well as my other girls, to comfort me and help fill that gap of emptiness.

My husband, Michael, had decided to go back to sea to deal with his pain, leaving me alone in a strange country with three little children and my grief.

Time is a great healer, or so they say. I'm not so sure that I readily believed those that had told me that.

Though time does heal, more than anything, it was God coming into my life, making all things new, including me.

He healed me; He provided for me; He alone can bring good out of the darkest situations.

CHAPTER 6

# The Nightmares

I'm not sure how old Mikaela was when I became aware of her nightmares. She was very young, but able to articulate her words.

She would awake from her sleep crying and often screaming. When I went to her, in between her sobs, she would ask me the same question, "Mummy, was it you standing at the end of my bed with a knife?"

I would comfort her and tell her how silly that dream was, that I loved her and would never want to hurt her.

I can't tell you the number of times she awoke with that same dream and question. I never fully understood what was behind that dream until years later.

Mikaela was fourteen at the time and had a friend sleeping over. She hadn't mentioned the dream for a few years and I'd forgotten about it until this night. I was passing her bedroom door and overheard her speaking to her friend telling her about her dream, which was obviously still occurring. It shocked and deeply affected me that she was

That night I cried out to God asking Him what this dream meant. For the first time, I clearly understood its meaning. A spirit of death had attached itself to Mikaela in the womb because of the intention to abort. It wasn't me she was seeing at the end of her bed, but this spirit.

With the authority God gives us as His children, I broke the power of that spirit off my daughter's life and she was never bothered by that dream again. This fact was verified years later when I eventually shared with Mikaela about the almost abortion.

That time came when I felt that I needed to tell Mikaela. It was a very hard thing for me to do, to tell her what I once intended to do to her. But God, in His grace and infinite mercy, softened her heart and her reaction truly blessed me.

When I shared with her how God had divinely intervened, she said, "Well, Mum, that just makes me feel so special. It shows me that God intended for me to be born and has a purpose for me."

When I look at Mikaela now, I am so truly grateful that she was born. She is beautiful, talented, extremely artistic, strong-willed and tenacious. She has a soft, kind, loving and compassionate heart, and truly cares about people.

Mikaela turned forty on her last birthday. She has a husband, four children and two grandchildren, none of which would be here, but for the grace of God.

How truly blessed I am that God chose to reveal to me that she was not just a mass of cells, tissue and blood vessels, but a real living person, a baby, no matter how tiny and at what stage of development.

From the moment of conception, everything that we are, will be, and become, is already written on our DNA. From the moment of conception, we have a God-given spirit and a destiny.

CHAPTER 7

# The Survivors

The nightmares suffered by Mikaela, due to the abortion intent, are not an isolated incident. I was amazed by the many and varied stories I came across during my investigations. I have included just a few of these stories to reinforce the point that abortion has far reaching consequences to everyone concerned.

The main objective of this chapter is to bring to light the fact that babies in the womb, no matter how unformed they are as yet, are aware, not by the intellect of the mind, but by their God-given spirit.

The following stories will highlight this truth.

## JA's Story

Many babies miraculously survive abortion attempts. This first story belongs to a woman I will refer to as JA. JA's mother, when she was 19, had an affair with a married man. She became pregnant and at six weeks, he, the married man and father of the baby, aided her in her attempt to have an abortion. The abortion attempt somehow failed and the baby survived. When JA was born, her mother tried to give her away, and when that didn't work, she neglected her. When JA was about six weeks old, her grandfather came and took her, and her grandparents brought her up.

JA relates, that from a very young age, she experienced overwhelming feelings of being unwanted. This made no sense to her since her grandparents loved her and doted on her, and she had no physical remembrance of her mother's neglect since she had been too young. But these feelings of being unloved, being unworthy of love, and a heavy burden of sadness, refused to subside and instead intensified as she grew older. By age twelve, the feelings turned into depression and by fourteen, suicidal thoughts developed.

On reaching fifteen, she experienced the first of many admissions to mental health institutions for attempted suicide and self-harm. The years following were extremely turbulent ones; those same feelings and emotions hung over and affected every part of JA's life. She met her husband-to-be at age 20. He was a medical student with a keen interest in alternative therapies. In an attempt to help her find answers to her malady, he suggested they might try some guided relaxation therapy.

Lying down, JA was encouraged into a deep state of relaxation. Although she was fully conscious and in complete control of her faculties, she was deeply relaxed. Whilst in this relaxed state, the young man asked her a question, "Why do you keep hurting yourself?" What came out of JA's mouth both shocked and startled both of them. She answered him, "Why wouldn't I when my mother tried to kill me."

He quickly ventured another question, "How did your mother try to kill you?" JA immediately replied, "She had an abortion when she was pregnant with me and it didn't work." Suddenly, with the voicing of those statements, she felt a huge weight lift off of her. She sat bolt upright and exclaimed, "That's it! That's the answer!" They were both stunned and taken aback at this revelation.

Only four people had previously known about the abortion attempt up till that moment – her mother and father, the abortionist and her. Her grandparents did not know, and up till that time JA had not met her father, or the abortionist who had tried to kill her, and her mother certainly wasn't telling.

JA would only have been the size of a thumbnail at the time of the abortion. But, as tiny as she was, she had a heartbeat, and she had a God-given spirit.

No living person had given her this information, but it was as though she had always known it, within her spirit, and it was the reason she had suffered those deep, destructive feelings of not being wanted, feeling unworthy to live.

As tiny as she was at the time, she had, somehow miraculously escaped the abortionists curette tool without any physical defects. But the effects upon her psychologically and emotionally were deep and far reaching.

Although it was a turning point for JA, it was not the end of her trauma. When she confronted her mother with this new found revelation, her mother vehemently denied it and kept up the pretense until sometime later when JA decided to look for and find her father. She shared the news with her mother, hoping her mother might be happy for her. Instead, there was a stony silence on the other end of the receiver. JA had barely hung up when her mother called her back. Worried that the father might tell JA about the abortion attempt, her mother confessed the truth, that she had in fact tried to abort her. Sadly, for JA, her mother retained her stance of pro-choice and never did apologize to her.

## Elizabeth's Story

There is an old saying, "Sticks and stones may break my bones, but names will never hurt me." It's an untrue statement that we as children would often chant to one another, delivered in a sing-song voice after some mean or spiteful words had pierced our young hearts.

The truth is that we eventually recover from broken bones, but words have a destructive power that we sometimes never recover from.

Such was the case for Elizabeth for many years. Her mother had often said to her, "I really didn't want you, but now that I have you, I love you." Although Elizabeth's mum meant for her daughter to hear the emphasis on the second part of that statement, it was the first part that impacted her young mind and soul. As a result, there was a nagging doubt that remained for many years as to the genuineness and sincerity of being loved and wanted. Even though love was demonstrated by her mum and family, it was never sufficient to remove the power of those words, "I really didn't want you".

Elizabeth understood the logics of the circumstances surrounding her mother's life at the time of the attempted abortion. Her mother was forty-five and already had a 17-year-old, a 9-year-old and a 2-year-old to look after. She also had a bedridden mother, and a sister with her child living in their home with them. Elizabeth's father was fifty and worked in the Tanneries, bringing home a very minimal basic wage. Life would have been hard, and then to find out another child was on the way would not have been welcome news. All of these facts together would go a long way to explaining why a normally loving mother would be driven to such desperate means to prevent an unwanted pregnancy.

Elizabeth loved her mum and chose to forgive and honor her. But wanting to, and choosing to understand the situation logically, did nothing to heal the pain of the wound in her heart.

Good health was a benefit that seemed to evade Elizabeth, in fact, she was dogged by ill health for most of her adult life, some of which was life-threatening.

In her early twenties though, something more sinister began raising its head. Elizabeth became aware of an irrational fear of being poisoned. This persisted and worsened for some years. At one time when she was quite ill, she insisted that the doctor test her for poisoning. Where had this secret fear come from? She discovered the answer to that question about five years ago.

An elderly cousin came to visit one day for lunch; a lady that Elizabeth rarely saw. After lunch, as they walked in the garden, the cousin proceeded to tell Elizabeth a story that had obviously bothered her for many years. She related an incident when she (the cousin as a young woman) had come to visit for a weekend. It was at the time when Elizabeth's mother was pregnant with her. During that weekend, an uncle arrived with a bottle of 'brew' of some kind which he gave to Elizabeth's mother to drink, with the express purpose of aborting the baby. The cousin went on to say that Elizabeth's mother became very ill as a result. But despite jumping off of chairs and other means, the abortion failed.

Suddenly, so many things began to make sense to Elizabeth. Like pieces of a jigsaw puzzle fitting into place and connecting; the years of ill health and the fear of being poisoned; perhaps also, the loss of two of Elizabeth's babies may have been due to the damage done by the poison going through her tiny body whilst in the womb.

Are babies aware of what is happening to them whilst in the womb? Medical science is proving more and more today that this is so.

An interesting fact that Elizabeth shared is that it became known that for centuries, different cultures have conducted practices of reading specific topical themes during pregnancy, with a view to improving the unborn child's aptitude in that area, desiring the child to excel in those skills in a particular career chosen by their parents – a practice they obviously have found to work.

Elizabeth is convinced that the experience of what happened to her whilst in the womb has had a lasting effect and influence upon her life.

About the same time of the revelation shared by her cousin, Elizabeth attended a Priceless Life dinner where she watched and was deeply touched by a dance three young women performed. The dance depicted a baby trying to be born and hold onto life. Watching this performance greatly impacted Elizabeth's life and started a chain of events way beyond anything she could possibly have foreseen. On her way home after the dinner that night, Elizabeth asked God that if there was any meaning to what she had experienced whilst watching that dance, that He would reveal it to her. He showed her a picture of herself in the womb at the time when she was fighting for life.

God used these experiences to place a purpose within Elizabeth's heart. She developed an overwhelming urge, as well as an ability, to write a program on life within the womb during each trimester. The teachings are specifically for the benefit of women and girls in developing cultures, and include teachings on morality and relationships. Presently, the program is being used in the Philippines, East Timor and Argentina.

How wonderful our God is, in that He alone can turn circumstances around in such a way as to bring so much good out of something so potentially bad.

With a fresh insight and understanding that had come from her cousin's revelation and the divine experiences of that night, Elizabeth was able to forgive her mother and her uncle in a much deeper way. For only in forgiving them could her own inner healing be complete.

## Gianna's Story

I decided to include Gianna Jessen's story in this chapter of my book, as she is most definitely a survivor and an incredible woman. Unlike the other women whose stories I have included, I have never actually spoken to, or corresponded with Gianna. But I have read and researched Gianna's story from many articles on the internet and YouTube.

Her story begins when Gianna's 17-year-old mother was 7 ½ months pregnant and decided to have an abortion by Saline injection. There is no legal time limit for abortion in America.

The Saline is injected into the womb and literally burns the baby inside and out over a period of 24 hours.

In Gianna's case, she survived the abortion attempt and was born alive (all 2lbs of her) after 18 hours.

A nurse called the emergency services and Gianna was taken to hospital where she spent the first three months of her life in an incubator, before being placed in emergency foster care.

At 17 months old, Gianna was diagnosed with cerebral palsy, due to her brain being starved of oxygen during the termination attempt. She was placed in the care of a foster mother who was later to become her adoptive grandmother.

Gianna says, "The doctors did not expect me to live, but I did; they said I would not be able to hold up my head, and I did; they said I would not sit up, crawl, or walk, but I did." By age three, with the help of her foster mother, she was walking with leg braces and a frame, all by the grace of God.

Gianna was bullied and teased unmercifully at school because of the physical effects of cerebral palsy. One day, when she was sixteen, a stranger came up to her and told her that children with disabilities were a burden on society. She smiled at the woman because she knew in her heart that this was not true. Gianna remembered that she had a tremendous fear of fire, which she felt was due to the burning of the saline.

She would ask her adoptive mother why she had this disability, and was told it was because she had a traumatic premature birth. Something within Gianna was never satisfied with that answer, so she kept asking. Then one day when she was twelve, her adoptive mother thought it was time for her to know the truth.

She began telling her that her biological mother was young and without hope, but before she could say any more, Gianna blurted out, "I was aborted, right?" Her adoptive mother confirmed this was so. Somehow Gianna just seemed to know it. She remembers feeling calm and she said, "It must have been the Lord, because I didn't freak out. I totally believe that the Lord Jesus spared my life and I would not be walking today if it were not for the grace of God and the power of Christ. I know that when you need God to be able to walk every day, you know that God is real."

Gianna totally forgives her biological mother and does not dwell on feelings of rejection.

'The 11th Hour', an American TV program, sponsored a Sanctity of Life Rally in Modesto, where Gianna was to tell her story.

Louise Shatswell, the producer of 'The 11th Hour', said that she hoped those who heard Gianna would be touched by her story and that their eyes would be opened to the reality of life at that stage of life. She went on to say, "I don't believe the majority of people who get abortions are really informed about what they are doing. Gianna is a living example of an unborn child actually being a child and not being a thing, a glob, an unidentified piece of nothing."

Gianna is quoted as saying, "My mother made a decision that she thought affected only her, yet every day I bear the results of that decision through my cerebral palsy. I'm not saying that in condemnation, but in truth.

It's ridiculous to think that our choices on a moment-by-moment basis only affect us. They always affect someone else, for good or ill."

Gianna is a full-time disability rights and anti-abortion campaigner, which began when she was fourteen. She lives in Nashville, Tennessee and travels the world talking about her experience. Gianna has spoken and told her story before many of the world's 'powers to be'. She met President Bush in 2002 and has appeared before Congress, speaking against partial-birth abortion in 1999 and in support of the Born-Alive Infants Protection Act in 2000. Whilst in London, Gianna spoke at the House of Lords in support of the British charity 'Alive and Kicking', which campaigns to eliminate abortion on the grounds of disability.

In 2008, Gianna spoke at Queens Hall, Parliament House, Victoria, Australia, on the eve of the debate to decriminalize abortion in Victoria. She has been to Australia many times, before and since, to speak in defense of the unborn. One of the questions that Gianna asks the members of parliament and of Congress of various nations is, "If abortion is about women's rights, then what were mine? There was no radical feminist screaming for my rights that day."

Gianna is an incredible woman, she is an accomplished song writer and singer, as well as an eloquent speaker.

For someone who was never supposed to walk, let alone live, in 2004, she ran her first marathon in seven and a half hours, and in 2006, she ran in the London 26-mile-long marathon for the 'Stars Organization for Cerebral Palsy'.

These were definitely not easy accomplishments, due to her disability, but Gianna probably approached them with the same tenacity, strength and determination that she has displayed from her unexpected birth and through every obstacle she has faced in her life since. Rightfully so, Gianna gives all the glory to God. She was marked for death even before she was born, but God had another

plan and purpose for her.

Mother Teresa said of Gianna, "God is using Gianna to remind the world that each human being is precious to Him. It is beautiful to see the strength of the love of Jesus which He has poured into her heart. My prayer for Gianna, and for all who listen to her, is that this message of God's love will put an end to abortion with the power of love."

One interesting, yet horrifying fact that Gianna mentions in her story, is that if the abortionist had been on duty when she was born alive, he would have 'finished her off', as she puts it. But she was born early in the morning, before he came on duty. When the nurse saw that she was still alive, she sent for an ambulance.

The irony is that the abortionist who tried to kill her had to sign her birth certificate.


*Information for this article obtained from the following resources:

Daily Telegraph

BlessedCause.com

Giannajesson.com

YouTube

CHAPTER 8

# Redemptive Healing

I fully believe that the majority of women who have had an abortion were uninformed and therefore unaware of the magnitude of what they were doing. One of the fundamental parts in the foundation for healing is learning to forgive ourselves. We can only fully do this with the help of God.

The stories in this chapter belong to precious women who have been through the agony of abortion. Each story is completely unique and different in itself, yet the after effects are the same – pain, regret, remorse, sadness, guilt, sense of loss and emotional damage. Each of these women have suffered the devastating consequences of abortion. But each have also found the grace and forgiveness of a loving God who has healed and delivered them.

## Karen's Story

Karen was very young when she arrived with her mother in Australia. Her mother was running away from her husband, Karen's father, whom she'd left in New Zealand. They had married after her mother became pregnant, but, their relationship had not worked out and she'd come to Australia to start a new life. They later divorced.

Her mother then met and married a man who Karen grew up believing to be her father. Karen couldn't understand why this man she called dad treated her so differently from her younger siblings and why he began sexually abusing her.

When Karen was thirteen, her mother told her he was not her real father, that her real father lived in New Zealand. Suddenly, some of the inward questions that had tormented her made sense.

At sixteen, Karen left home. She drifted between youth refuges and hostels, sleeping wherever she could find shelter. Life had not been too kind to her at this time in her young life.

During the ensuing years, she became involved in the 'bikie', come alcohol and drug scene'. She was in a relationship with one of the bikers, a man called Mick, when she became pregnant. Karen was 23 by this time, and, being tired of her life as it was, she found she was happy to be pregnant. Unfortunately, Mick did not share her elation. On the contrary, he became very angry. His parents were strict Catholics who, apparently, were unaware of his lifestyle, and would have greatly disapproved. They were also unaware that Karen and he were living together. He was so desperate to keep it that way that he strongly insisted that Karen have an abortion.

Karen kept delaying the abortion in the hope he would change his mind, showing him ultrasound pictures at fourteen weeks in which you could clearly see a baby. His response was, "Very nice, but we can't keep it."

She was 18 weeks pregnant when she finally submitted to his will.

Karen went to an abortion clinic, and under what is termed twilight sedation, her baby was aborted.

After the abortion she sat in a small room where a middle-aged, stern-faced nurse took down some details. The face of this nurse is deeply imprinted in Karen's memory. She kept asking the nurse if the baby was a boy or a girl. The nurse brushed aside her questions, insisting it was only blood product. She barely looked up as she continued writing, as though she wanted to avoid visual contact, not wanting to connect with Karen's eyes.

Karen went home feeling empty. For the first time, she realized that she was a mother – a mother without a baby. She was deeply affected within the realm of her soul, and would continue to be so for some time.

Thirty-six hours later, Karen was curled up on her bed in tremendous pain, experiencing hot and cold sweats. Mick took her to the hospital. After a few hours, they sent her home with Panadeine. Three days later in the early hours of the morning, suffering delirium and the very real possibility that she might die, Karen was again in hospital. This time she was left on a hospital trolley, in a corridor, for six hours. Whilst lying there, Karen had an urge to bear down. She somehow managed to get off the trolley and into the toilet where she passed the remaining parts of her baby into the toilet bowl. The nurse, who responded to the alarm bell, made Karen scoop the baby parts into a plastic bag herself.

They took her to surgery where they performed a D & C on her, which involved using a curette to scrape any remaining baby parts from her womb. They sent her home the next day.

Karen broke off the relationship with Mick two months later. Sometime after this, in New Zealand, she met and became involved with Marcus and became pregnant again. Marcus, unlike Mick, was happy about the pregnancy.

Karen was still addicted to drugs, and, when she was four months pregnant, her unborn baby girl was diagnosed with a condition called Microcephaly. In layman's terms, the growth of the baby's brain is stunted.

Two months later, after an accumulation of circumstances, Karen and Marcus were at the home of a Pastor who, after leading them both to Jesus, prayed for them and their unborn baby. God did some wonderful, powerful miracles. Both Karen and Marcus were mightily touched by God. Karen was delivered from her addiction to heavy drugs and alcohol.

God touched her precious baby with a healing miracle too and she was completely delivered of Microcephaly. The doctors continued to monitor the baby, doing regular scans on her brain, but, four weeks after that prayer, she was fully discharged from their care as completely well and whole.

The doctors were unable to explain what had happened.

Karen was still half expecting her baby to be affected in some way, due to the drugs that she was taking whilst expecting her, but by the grace of God, this precious baby was born perfectly normal.

Many people, mostly complete strangers, were touched by the serenity that emanated from this child.

She is now a 23-year-old married woman, bright, intelligent and beautiful.

A little while after Karen first became a Christian, an incident happened that brought to the surface some partially buried feelings. A grandmother, during a church fellowship meeting, remarked about seeing her granddaughter's ultrasound pictures of her baby. Not knowing Karen's past, she commented that the pictures so clearly revealed that this was a baby, and that she failed to understand how anyone could possibly justify abortion.

There's an old saying that I believe to be so true, and that is that God sometimes allows our cup to be bumped just to let us see what's in it, and perhaps, what may need to be dealt with.

As Karen left that meeting and went home that afternoon, she realized how much grief and pain she still carried on the inside of her due to her abortion.

The incident brought back the memory of how she herself had had an ultrasound, and had looked at the pictures of her baby. This memory caused deep wells of grief to erupt within her.

She cried out to God, telling Him that she could not carry this burden alone anymore. God heard the cry of her heart that afternoon, and He led her to open her Bible. As she randomly opened it, her eyes fell on the very Scripture He wanted her to read – Ezekiel 16:4-6, 8.

God brought healing to Karen's heart and this Scripture brought her great peace, for every word of this Scripture shows us that God cares for those aborted babies and takes them to Himself.

One day when we go to be with God in heaven, those children will be waiting for us, each and every one of them.

## Sally's Story

Sally was taught independence early in life, having spent most of her learning years in boarding school. She continued her independence after leaving school, getting a job interstate away from the influence of her family. Her life revolved around parties and excessive drinking, which seemed a perfectly normal existence to her at the time; that's just what people did, worked and had fun.

Sally's two elder sisters had been unable to have children for some reason and had adopted. She was twenty-five by this time and found herself wondering if she herself would be able to have children. Without thinking of the consequences, Sally had unprotected sex for a while and did in fact become pregnant. Then came the decision of what to do next. Her options were: have the baby and adopt it out, have the baby and raise it with help from family, or, have an abortion. After much anxious deliberation, she came to the very hard and painful decision to have an abortion, with the thought that she could have children later when she was ready. After making this difficult decision, she became overwhelmed with remorse and sadness, with the fact that she could not turn back the clock and change her mind. It was done now and she had to live with the consequences. All she wanted now was to have a baby.

It was not long after this that Sally met her husband Frank and thought she would just get pregnant, but discovered that the IUD she'd had fitted after the abortion had damaged her fallopian tube. Owing to the state of her mind after the abortion, she hadn't had it checked.

Sally longed to have a child, and so, with the thought that she might never be able to, she started to drink even more. This put a real strain on their marriage and so they separated for a while. She went home to her parents and whilst there, started going to Alcoholics Anonymous in a desperate attempt to get her life back on track.

Prior to them separating, a friend from a local pub became a Christian and started to share with them about Jesus.

It took a year before they got back together, but when they did, there was a resolve in both of them for change. They decided to go with their friend to church and eventually asked Jesus into their hearts and lives. Sally remembers crying out, "Lord, if you are real, please help me." She heard the Scripture, "Come to me, all you who labor and are heavy laden, and I will give you rest." (Matthew 11:28) Oh, how she longed for that rest. She heard how Jesus died on the cross for our sins and that He took the burden of sin for us, so that we could be set free. How much she needed to hear that. How much she needed that freedom. Jesus came into her life at her invitation and there was a deep reassurance in her heart that she had been forgiven. From that moment on, she fell in love with Jesus as her Lord and Savior.

There were many months of weeping, prayer and deliverance as their lives got transformed. They gave their hearts so completely that this beautiful couple went on to help and minister to many people over the years who were lost as they had been.

They both still desperately wanted children and Sally did become pregnant, but unfortunately had a miscarriage after three months. Of course, this was extremely devastating to both of them and took time to get over, but it created a determination in Sally to press in to God in prayer. Sally received a peace and quiet assurance in her heart that one day she would be a mother.

A few years later, through 'Assisted Fertility', the Lord answered their prayers and Frank and Sally had twin boys. They are the absolute joy of their lives. The doctor called them miracle babies.

In the depths of Sally's heart is that same quiet assurance that one day, those two other precious babies will be there to greet her when she enters into heaven, our eternal home.

## Susan's Story

Susan grew up as a Christian, always attending church and Christian schools. At 12, she immigrated to Australia from Italy with her parents.

In the Catholic schools she attended as well as in her home, sex education was considered a taboo subject never to be discussed. But behind the veil of respectability and morality that dominated the community in which she lived, Susan was well aware that sin abounded, even in her own family.

Susan met Ben, who was eventually to become her husband, in year 11 at high school. She had a deep love for God and she knew that God loved her, but perhaps because of the hypocrisy that surrounded her, she rebelled, and she and Ben became involved in a sexual relationship.

At age 22, they were both in university doing their separate degrees when Susan discovered that she was pregnant. Susan was terrified at the thought of her parents finding out. Her father, especially, was extremely strict and would likely cut her off financially. How then would she finish university? How would she live? Another thought terrified her – what would her community say? Her parents would be shamed. She could not put her parents through that disgrace.

Susan talked with Ben, and they discussed their options. He was very loving and caring, and said that whatever Susan decided to do, he would support her.

One day, as Susan was driving along the motorway, she saw a billboard. The words read, "Are you pregnant?" "Do you need help?" She knew she needed help. She hadn't yet made her mind up, and having no one else to turn to except Ben, she desperately needed to talk to someone who could give her advice. She decided that she would call them and make an appointment. A few days later, Ben drove her to the appointment. In her naivety, Susan did not realize that this was an abortion clinic. The wording on the billboard made it sound like it was some sort of pregnancy counselling organization. She did see a 'so-called' counsellor who asked her just a few questions. The woman asked her how far into the pregnancy she was. Susan told her that she was about four weeks. The only counselling that she received was to have an abortion. The counsellor told her that her problem would be solved and that she would be able to get back to her life, continue with her studies and all would be well. When Susan asked about procedures and about the baby, she was told that it was not a baby, just a mass of cells; it was too early to be anything else. Susan said to give her a week to think it over and talk with her boyfriend. The counsellor quickly told her she'd be five weeks pregnant by then and needed to get it done as soon as possible.

Two days later, after covering their tracks with their parents, Ben drove her to the clinic. She went under general anesthetic, but when she awoke she was told that the procedure hadn't worked. They had inserted the dilation rods but because her cervix was very small, she had not dilated enough for them to do the abortion. She had to keep the rods in overnight and come back the next day. Susan was extremely distraught. A strong feeling of conviction came upon her; she just knew in her gut that this was not right, but she didn't know what else to do. The next day she was back at the clinic where they continued with the abortion. Susan didn't handle the anesthetic too well, so she spent the whole day recovering at the clinic till 5pm when they closed. Ben didn't know what to do as Susan was still in and out of consciousness and vomiting. He drove around town, not daring to take her home in this state. It was quite late by the time he dropped her off, but at least by that time she was able to walk in-doors by herself.

Although on the surface, life seemed to get back to normal, some things were certainly not right within Susan. She felt very unsettled and couldn't concentrate on anything. Her studies suffered and she found she couldn't cope with her part-time job and had to give it up. She went to see the counsellor at the university to talk things over but had to admit she couldn't finish her degree. She couldn't seem to concentrate or do anything and fell into a depression. She would cry every day without knowing why she was crying; there seemed to be no joy left in her life. All this time Ben was very supportive. The doctor gave Susan depression medication, to which she had a bad reaction. This made her quite ill for a while, adding to the problem rather than helping.

All this time, Susan hadn't connected the depression with the abortion. It had been a few years since it happened and she had put it behind her and not thought about it since.

Ben and Susan married and were very happy, but the depression persisted. One day, they went for a long drive and talked over all that had happened in her life that may have led to the depression. They only briefly touched on the abortion issue, but straight after that talk the depression lifted.

They went on to have three children, but two years after the last child was born, the depression came back. Susan was having panic attacks and felt like she had no control over anything. One day, while she was in prayer about the situation, God spoke to her. He said, "The only thing that will get you through this is finding me."

That same year Susan's dad gave her an iPad for her birthday. After receiving that word from God, she decided to look for something spiritual on the internet and found a daily audio Bible. It takes you through the whole Bible in one year. Through that daily reading, Susan truly found God in a way she had never known Him before.

She went on to do a podcast study of Doctor Neil Anderson's book 'Restored, finding Freedom in Christ'. After reading the chapter on abortion, she finally realized that this was the probable cause of the depression she had suffered all this time. She and Ben put into practice what they had been learning from doing this study. They confessed, repented and consecrated themselves to Jesus. Life completely changed for them after that time – no more depression!

Not long after that, Susan once more heard God's voice. This time God said to her, "I want you to counsel women who have had an abortion." For a while Susan struggled with this instruction. She had three young children and a job that was a part of the family income. However, with Ben's approval, Susan went back to University for three years to study counselling, and then further specialized training in the area that she needed to counsel post abortive women.

One thing Susan remembers when she thinks back to sitting in the waiting room of that abortion clinic, and that was the faces of the other young women that were sitting there. She remembers the fear and uncertainty in their eyes. They were as desperate as she was. What they all needed, at that time, was love and guidance and real options. Now Susan is in the place where God has placed her, to be able to give that love and guidance, and especially to help bring healing to those women that are now where she once was.

## Mary's Story

Mary was born into a good Christian family. Although her parents were not well educated, they were hard-working people with strong moral values which they taught and imparted into their children. As a result, Mary and her siblings grew up with a keen awareness and understanding of right and wrong. There was not much in the way of financial security, yet there was, and still is, a close relationship between Mary and her siblings and a great respect and honor for their parents.

Mary grew up in the country where she developed a deep affection for the country life. Although her family moved around a lot during her childhood, they finally settled in a country coastal town where she finished high school.

It was here that Mary began to take an interest in boys. She was fifteen when she met her first real boyfriend who was a year older than her. They became good friends and were together for about five years. Mary was twenty when she discovered she was pregnant. She was very upset, ashamed and frightened at the thought of her parents finding out. She didn't want to bring shame on them and cause them to be disappointed in her. The thought of facing other family members and friends was almost as bad.

Mary's parents had high hopes for her. They envisioned her furthering her education and achieving something with her life. Being pregnant would undoubtedly eliminate those plans. After much agonizing, Mary decided her only way out was to have an abortion. Her boyfriend told her that he would support her in whatever she chose to do. Mary went to see her doctor who booked her into a clinic. She was shocked when the clinic rejected her on the grounds that they believed that she was too advanced. She was then referred to another clinic, where she was not given a general anesthetic and could feel quite a lot of discomfort during the abortion, but she was too afraid to say anything. It was an extremely traumatic experience.

Mary chose to move on with her life, attempting to put it all behind her. She broke off the relationship with her boyfriend as things were never the same after that.

She kept her secret for many years. Except for one or two very close friends, no one ever knew.

She also kept to herself the agonizing guilt, and very deep regret that she felt, until she finally gave her life over to Jesus Christ and experienced His love and forgiveness.

Mary relates, that although it may take time for our emotions to be completely healed, that sense of sorrow was no longer there, because she became aware that one day she will be reconciled with her child in heaven. That knowledge alone brings the deepest sense of joy and peace.

Mary later married. She has three children and three grandchildren whom she loves and adores. She also has a wonderful husband who loves and cares for her. She realizes how gracious God has been to her and how blessed she is, but Mary said, "If I could go back and change the decision that I made all those years ago, I would do it in a heartbeat. I am now aware of how precious life is, and the life of an unborn child is to be highly valued and never taken for granted."

Of course, we cannot go back to change decisions we've made in the past, but we can change our future by the choices we make now. We can have that same peace and assurance that Mary, Susan, Sally and Karen have. We can have that same healing, restoration and hope that they have. It can begin today!

CHAPTER 9

# The Light at the End of the Tunnel

One thing that always leaves me frustrated and exasperated is listening to someone describe a wonderful destination without telling me how to get there. I'm not talking about a geographical destination, but rather a solution to a problem perhaps, or something that might bring a tremendous change to my life and circumstances, or something that truly inspires me and lifts my spirit, but then, I'm left up in the air because they don't explain how to achieve it. They may be able to tell me what I need, but unless they tell me where to get it, their advice is of little use to me. I, most definitely, resolve not to do that. Hence, this last chapter is the light that, hopefully, shines upon the pathway that will lead you to 'the One' who heals and restores.

All of the stories I have included in this book are real life stories that belong to real people. With the help of each of these wonderful women, I have attempted to be as factual as possible. Each person's story is unique to them, yet, there is likely much within their stories that would relate to each one of us.

The common thread with each of these women is that their desperate circumstances revealed their desperate need.

That same need that is present in all of our lives, for a savior. The sad thing is, most of us have to go through many painful trials before we recognize that need.

At the same time though, the most wonderful thing is, God promises to bring good out of all of those trials. Each life represented in this book bears testament to that truth.

These women who have bravely shared their stories, have done so in the fervent hope that others might find that same peace, freedom and healing that they are now enjoying.

There is a good chance, since you are reading this book, that you might be in need of some of that peace, freedom and healing.

You may have travelled through life, up to this point in time, never knowing or believing that there is a God. I want to assure you, with all sincerity, that though you may not know Him, He has always known you, and that He believes in you. The Bible tells us that He formed us in our mother's womb. He knew each one of us before the foundation of the earth. He knows all the days allotted to us. He longs for us to acknowledge Him and to open up our hearts and invite Him in.

His love for us is unconditional. There is nothing about our lives that has ever been hidden from Him. He knows all of our secrets; He knows where we've come from and what we've done.

Yet, He loves us!

The Bible tells us that He knows the end from the beginning, which means that He already knew, even before we were born, everything that we would do.

Yet because of Jesus, He is so ready to forgive us and welcome us into His loving arms.

There is nothing that I can share with you with more honesty and sincerity than my own testimony, much of which I've already shared so far, but to continue:

Up till the time of deciding to go to Australia, I had suffered every kind of abuse that is known *as* abuse. A deep darkness had enveloped me that was closing in ever tighter, threatening to suffocate me. I had considered suicide many times. Early one morning, after a particularly dark time, I was on the very verge of acting on it. I had several open bottles of pills in front of me, which I'd made up my mind to swallow, when a thought, or really a question was dropped into my mind, "If you die, who will get your children?" It's as if time was suspended whilst that thought registered.

I felt comforted in the thought of my mum bringing up my children. But I knew that my mother-in-law, who was quite comfortably off financially, would do all in her power to make quite sure that she got them. Thankfully, the thought of her doing to my children what she had done to Michael, was enough to deter me.

Of course, I now know that it was God who dropped that question into my mind, and thankfully, He never allowed me to forget the answer.

What had started as an 'inspirational' idea to go to Australia seemed to blossom into a miracle, like someone had switched on a life support machine.

Michael's promises about changing and starting afresh when we moved to Australia, seemed to hold true. That first month, after we arrived, was the happiest time of our whole marriage. Michael would come home from work and we would all go as a family to the beach, which was just across the road from the hostel. It was a novelty to us to be so close to the sea, as we had lived in Coventry in England all of our lives. Coventry is right in the middle of the country. The sea is as far away east as it is west, and farther still north and south.

Everything was so fresh and new and exciting and Michael seemed as happy as I was. The children too were happy in their new school. It was like a dream come true.

We even managed to acquire a cheap little car on terms, so we could explore further afield. But, unfortunately, the car was both a blessing and a curse. Michael started making friends at work and began stopping off for a drink on his way home. At first it was one or two nights a week, but before too long it was every night, and within a short time, things deteriorated back to the way they had always been – excessive drinking and then abuse.

The beautiful dream came crashing down.

On top of all of this, Jason was sick, and no one seemed to know exactly what was wrong with him. He just seemed to be getting worse. I took him to a doctor that I'd found in the town one day. He was a young doctor but I felt confident that he seemed to know what he was talking about. I told him Jason's symptoms and he took some blood to test. I remember, as I walked with Jason up the hallway away from his surgery, that the doctor stood at his door and watched Jason walk. There were many things that I didn't understand at the time, that were apparent symptoms of the tumor that Jason was eventually diagnosed with. One of which was what this doctor was watching. Jason walked with his legs slightly apart, which was his body's way of compensating for the lack of balance caused by pressure on his brain.

There were other signs that, as a layman, I had not noticed *as* signs, such as: Jason slept with his eyes more open than closed, something he had always done from a baby, yet it never ceased to un-nerve me. This can also be because of pressure on the brain. Another sign of pressure on the brain was the way Jason would carry his head back, like he was looking at the sky. During the time he was so sick, I noticed that whenever I went over a bump with him in his pushchair, he would cry out, but because he was so young he couldn't tell me what was wrong.

I now understand that I couldn't have known what these symptoms and signs meant at the time. But at first, when I did find out, a great guilt overtook me and I beat myself up so many times telling myself that I should have known. This was a lie.

We suffer from much of this type of deception in the course of our lives. The reason is simply this, as well as having a wonderful loving God who wants to heal us and set us free, we also have an enemy. The devil is the *'inspirer'* of every wrong decision that we make, as well as the *'accuser'* after we make them, and are suffering the results or the consequences.

I am not advocating, by any means, the old saying, 'the devil made me do it'. On the contrary, God has given us a free will to choose, and we must make, and be responsible for, our own decisions. What I am saying is that he takes every opportunity to guide and influence our decisions, and he uses many ploys that we may unknowingly be open to.

The Bible says, "The thief *(the devil)* does not come except to steal, and to kill, and to destroy. I *(God)* have come that they may have life, and that they may have *it* more abundantly." (John 10:10 [emphasis added]) The devil is an expert at what he does, but thank God, for He is a greater expert.

Each of these women have openly shared about the painful circumstances surrounding their lives. As a result, each had deep open and weeping wounds, into which this enemy has been able to continually pour his poison of guilt, shame, and regret.

In the natural, we first have to clean a wound to get rid of all the gunk and dirt. Then it needs to be cleansed with antiseptic and antibiotics to get rid of the poison before the wound can even begin to heal. Otherwise, it will fester, get worse and the poison will spread. The same principles apply to our emotions, to our spirit and our soul. Nurses and doctors are well able to take care of our physical bodies, but only the Lord God Almighty can heal our hearts, our minds, our emotions and our spirit. As long as these wounds stay open, the devil will continue to torment and accuse.

Each of these women, myself, and many others, have found Jesus as our healer. He has gradually healed the painful memories, taken away that awful pain of regret, dealt with the guilt and the shame, so that the enemy has nowhere left to pour his poison. He has given us beauty for ashes, the oil of joy for mourning, and He has brought restoration and peace to our lives.

We have found Jesus as our Savior. We each have a hope and assurance in our hearts, that when we leave this world (whenever that may be) because we have made Him Lord of our lives, we will be with Him in Heaven and our lost little ones will be there waiting for us.

Jesus is the Good Shepherd who laid down His life for the sheep. He died for the sins of each one of us. For not one of us is without sin. The word 'sin' may sound like a religious word to you, but it simply means to break God's righteous laws, and every one of us has done that, probably many times in our lives.

God's laws are there for our benefit, to protect us from harming ourselves or others.

We needed a savior to stand in the gap for us. The Son of God chose to do that because He loves us.

He didn't have to; He chose to!

In response to that, we in turn need to make a choice.

At the beginning of this book, I mentioned about the choices we make in life. Some good, some not so good and some we live to regret. Please, don't live one more moment in regret.

Jesus is the light at the end of the tunnel, but rather than an end, it's really a beginning. He is the one who can heal your pain, give you peace, restore your life, and give you a hope and a future.

I promised not to leave you up in the air without showing you the way. In fact, the whole book has really been about the way.

The Bible tells us in Romans 10:9, 10: "If you confess with your mouth the Lord Jesus and believe in your heart that God has raised Him from the dead, you will be saved. For with the heart one believes unto righteousness, and with the mouth confession is made unto salvation."

If you have related to the testimonies that you have read, perhaps because you are suffering in the same way, why not give Jesus an opportunity to set you free? Your life can also be a beautiful testimony.

You have nothing to lose and everything to gain.

The Bible in Revelations 3:20 says, "Behold, I stand at the door and knock. If anyone hears My voice and opens the door, I will come in to him and dine with him, and he with Me. *(Restore him)*" (Emphasis added)

Jesus stands at the door of our hearts wanting to come in.

Opening the door and inviting Him in is as simple and easy as saying a prayer such as this one:

**Dear Lord Jesus,**
**I confess that I've made many mistakes and broken your righteous laws.**
**I'm sorry Lord, and I ask you to forgive me.**
**I believe you died in my place so that I could be forgiven.**
**I open up the door to my heart and ask you to come in.**
**Help me to follow you with all my heart.**
**Please heal me, restore me and make me new.**
**Amen**

If you have said this prayer and been sincere in your heart, a wonderful thing has just happened. Having asked Jesus into our heart, the Bible says that we are a new creation in Christ, the old has passed away and the new has come. You are a new person with a new beginning.

Today is the first day of the rest of your life!

If you want to experience the healing spoken of in this book, I encourage you not to stop here, but to find a Bible believing church where other Christians can support you, pray for you, and help you to find healing. They will also encourage you to pray, which is just talking to God. And to read the Bible, which is God's way to talk to you.

Often, the emotional trauma we have suffered can lead to physical sickness. The Bible tells us that Jesus bore our sicknesses as well as our guilt and shame. Therefore, healing belongs to us as Christians.

My prayer for everyone who has read this book and said this prayer, is that you grow in faith, receive complete healing and restoration, and that the joy of the Lord fills your hearts to overflowing.

I have included a page of Scripture references that will be of great help and benefit to you as you read them. I have also included a resource page. The resource page has links that contain useful information that you may also find helpful. There are also links to organizations that have counselling facilities.

CHAPTER 10

# A Word to Christian Women

I dedicate this chapter to those women who were already Christians before reading this book, who have had an abortion at some stage in their lives and have not as yet found or experienced the healing described within these pages. There are many, I'm sure, that fit that description.

The biggest stumbling block to receiving healing, I believe, is accepting God's forgiveness. Forgiveness has to be accepted by faith in His Word. If you have confessed and repented, even if you were a Christian when you had the abortion and knew that what you were doing was wrong but have since repented, then you can know for sure that you are forgiven, for God does not lie. 1 John 1:9 tells us, "If we confess our sins, He is faithful and just to forgive us *our* sins and to cleanse us from all unrighteousness."

The person we are least willing to forgive is ourselves. Most Christians realize that they need to forgive others, but have the greatest difficulty forgiving themselves. We have an inward need to be punished for our mistakes, and so, we subconsciously punish ourselves.

Truth number one is that Jesus already took the punishment on our behalf to pay for 'all' of our sins and mistakes, and He paid 'in full'. Not accepting Jesus' grace and forgiveness is like saying His death wasn't enough to pay for *my* sin.

Truth number two is that God says in the Lord's prayer, "Forgive us our sins as *'we'* forgive those that sin against us". It's equally important that we forgive ourselves.

Forgiveness is a choice of our will. Choosing to forgive ourselves, or accepting forgiveness from God, has nothing to do with our 'feelings'. Whether we 'feel' forgiven or not, it's all about faith and believing His Word.

Abortion is a sin, but it is not beyond the blood of Jesus and the cross. He chose to forgive you and accept you when you first came to Him, knowing what you had done and what you would do, because He loves you. We are all sinners working out our salvation with fear and trembling, none worse than another.

It's as we choose to forgive that God gradually heals our emotions that have been deeply hurt and wounded.

I encourage you to ask the Holy Spirit to help you. He is our helper.

We need to speak the truth to ourselves, to negate the lies that we may have believed.

The truth is we are blood-bought, blood-washed children of God, whose sins have been removed from us as far away as the east is from the west, thrown into the sea of forgetfulness.

So, if God forgives and forgets, then why shouldn't we?

If He doesn't condemn us, then we should not condemn ourselves.

A wonderful truth that always encourages me is that when I asked Jesus to be my Lord and Savior, He not only forgave the sins I'd committed up till that point in time, but also all the sins I may still commit and repent of (whilst in this mortal body) till the day I go to be with Him.

Through the precious blood of Jesus, He has made a way for you and me to be forgiven. Accept His forgiveness, forgive yourself and receive healing and release, and live your life powerful and purposeful.

Be assured, precious woman of God, that every baby, no matter at what stage of development, is alive and with Jesus.

Our babies await us in heaven!

# Scriptural References:

Isaiah 61:1

"The Spirit of the Lord God is upon Me, because the Lord has anointed me to preach good tidings to the poor; He has sent me to heal the broken hearted, to proclaim liberty to the captives, and the opening of the prison to those who are bound".

Isaiah 41:10

'Fear not, for I am with you; Be not dismayed, for I am your God. I will strengthen you, Yes, I will help you, I will uphold you with My righteous right hand'.

1 Peter 2:24

Who Himself bore our sins in His own body on the tree, that we, having died to sins, might live for righteousness – by whose stripes you were healed.

Psalm 107:19

Then they cried out to the Lord in their trouble, and He saved them out of their distresses.

Romans 3:22,23

Even the righteousness of God, through faith in Jesus Christ, to **all** and on **all** who believe. For there is no difference; 23 for **all** have sinned and fall short of the glory of God.

Romans 6:23

For the wages of sin is death, but the gift of God is eternal life in Christ Jesus our Lord.

1 John 1:9,10

If we confess our sins, He is faithful and just to forgive us our sins and to cleanse us from **all** unrighteousness. 10 if we say that we have not sinned, we make Him a liar, and His Word is not in us.

Romans 5:2

Therefore, having been justified by faith, we have peace with God through our Lord Jesus Christ.  Psalm 30:2

O Lord my God, I cried out to you, and you healed me.

Isaiah 53:5

But He was wounded for our transgressions, He was bruised for our iniquities; The chastisement for our peace was upon Him, and by His stripes we are healed.

Psalm 103:2-4

Bless the Lord, O my soul, and forget not all His benefits: who forgives all your iniquities, Who heals all your diseases, Who redeems your life from destruction, Who crowns you with lovingkindness and tender mercies.

Psalm 147:3

He heals the broken-hearted and binds up their wounds.

Philippians 4:6,7

Be anxious for nothing, but in everything by prayer and supplication, with thanksgiving, let your requests be made known to God; and the peace of God, which surpasses all understanding, will guard you hearts and minds through Christ Jesus.

Psalm 34:18

The Lord is near to those who have a broken heart, and saves such as have a contrite spirit.

Deuteronomy 31:6

Be strong and of good courage, do not fear or be afraid of them; for the Lord your God, He is the One who goes with you. He will not leave you nor forsake you.

2 Timothy 1:7

For God has not given us a spirit of fear, but of power and of love and a sound mind.

Ephesians 2:8

For by grace you have been saved through faith, and that not of yourselves; it is the gift of God.

## Helpful Resources & Associations

Below are some links to sites that could be helpful to you in your journey to healing. You will also find links with information about organizations where you will find support if you are in need of it.

http://blogs.thegospelcoalition.org/kevindeyoung/2014/01/22/how-god-healed-me-from-my-abortion/

http://www.patheos.com/blogs/bristolpalin/2015/01/nine-celebrities-who-have-spoken-out-about-the-horrors-and-regret-of-their-abortions/

http://www.rachelsvineyard.org/PDF/Articles/Even%20Famous%20Faces%20Hide%20-%20LifeLines.pdf

http://www.gotquestions.org/abortion-healing-recovery.html

http://choicesoflife.com.au/healing_after_abortion.php

http://www.infg.org/

http://www.littlethings.com/kimberly-henderson-abortion/

Below links to organizations you may find help with counselling are:

info@pricelesslifecentre.org.au

pcl.org.au

## ABOUT THE AUTHOR

Ann Taylor was born in Coventry, England in 1946. She emigrated to Australia in 1974 with her first husband, and three children. Over the years, Ann has ministered to women in various capacities. She presently leads the Women's ministry at Victory Life Church, Toowoomba, Queensland.

Ann's passion is to see women healed and set free. Her own traumatic past has given her an understanding and compassion for the broken. She felt inspired and compelled by God to write this book for the many women that have been broken by abortion. It is His will and desire that through this book they might find healing, forgiveness and restoration.